Archaeopteryx

Rhea

Ostrich

1

Emu

Cassowary

Kiwi

2

Crested grebe

Macaroni penguin

Albatross

Antarctic petrel

Gannet

Blue-footed booby

Great frigatebird

Cormorant

Anhinga

Brown pelican

White pelican

Trumpeter swan

Nene (Hawaiian goose)

Canada goose

Snow goose

7

Hooded merganser

Mallard

Pintail

Wood duck

Flamingo

Great blue heron

9

Snowy egret

White ibis

Roseate spoonbill

Marabou stork

White stork

King vulture

11

Osprey

Andean condor

Bald eagle

12

Harpy eagle

Goshawk

African vulture

13

Golden eagle

Sparrowhawk

Rough-legged hawk

Kite

Secretary-bird

Peregrine falcon

15

Caracara

Pheasant

Willow ptarmigan

Prairie-Chicken

Ruffed grouse

California quail

Wild turkey

Whooping crane

Crowned-Crane

18

Sandhill crane

Indian bustard

Long-billed curlew

Sandpiper

Phalarope

Oystercatcher

Avocet

Golden plover

Killdeer

California gull

Royal tern

Skua

22

Skimmer

Atlantic puffin

Loon

23

Pigeon

Turtle-dove

Blue-and-yellow macaw

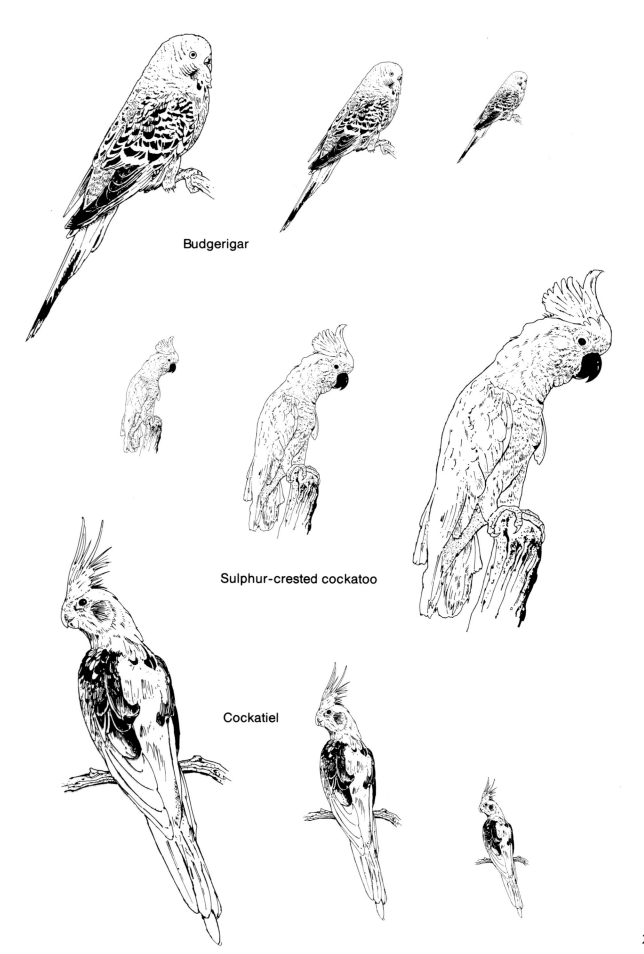

Budgerigar

Sulphur-crested cockatoo

Cockatiel

25

Roadrunner

Great horned owl

Spotted owl

26

Snowy owl

Hermit (a type of hummingbird)

Kingfisher

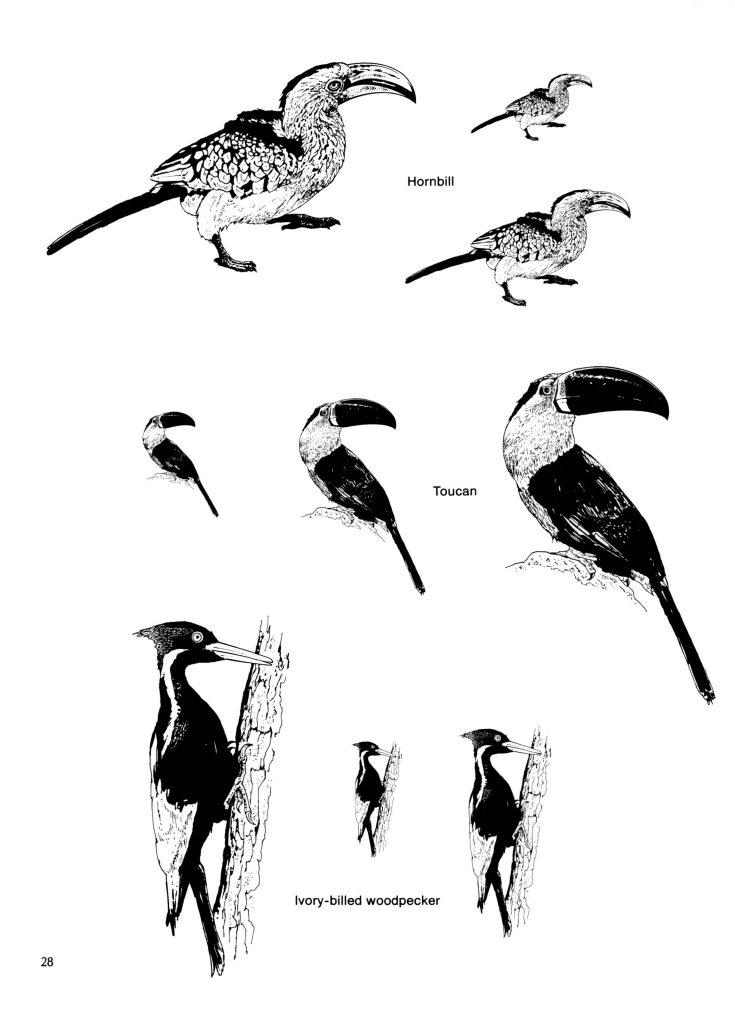

Hornbill

Toucan

Ivory-billed woodpecker

28

Raven

Blue jay

Shrike

29

American robin

Bluebird

Mockingbird

Myna

Starling

Nightingale

Cactus wren

Canary

Sparrow

Cardinal

Oriole